Getting Ready for School

by Katherine Scraper

I need to know these words.

backpack

bucket

bus

chore

horse

uniforms

How do you get ready
for school? How did boys
and girls get ready for school
long ago?

Did boys and girls get ready the same way that you do? Read this book to find out.

Some boys and girls put on **uniforms**. Do you put on a uniform?

These girls ▶ wear uniforms to school.

Some boys and girls put
on uniforms long ago, too.
These boys put on uniforms.

▲ These boys wore uniforms to school.

Some girls and boys do **chores** before school. This girl feeds her dog before school. Do you do chores before school?

▲ This girl does a chore before school.

Boys and girls did chores before school long ago, too. Many boys and girls lived on farms. The boys and girls helped on the farm.

▲ These boys did chores before school.

Some boys and girls take lunch to school. This boy is making his lunch. He will put his lunch in his **backpack**.

◄ This boy takes his lunch to school.

Boys and girls made their lunches long ago, too. Many boys and girls put their lunches in **buckets**.

▲ This boy took a bucket to school.

How do you get to school? Some boys and girls walk to school. Some boys and girls ride a bike. Some boys and girls ride a **bus**.

◀ A bus is one way to get to school.

▲ These girls walk to school.

Many boys and girls walked to school long ago, too. Some boys and girls rode **horses**. Boys and girls did not ride a bus long ago.

▲ This boy rode a horse to school.

Today, all boys and girls must go to school. Long ago, many boys and girls did not go to school.

▲ Many boys and girls stayed home to work.

These boys and girls helped their families. Some boys and girls helped sell things. Many boys and girls did not learn to read.

▲ These boys stayed home to sell things.

Boys and girls get ready for school today. Boys and girls got ready for school long ago. How do you get ready for school?